Liquid Song:
a little book of longing

poems by

Adeline Carrie Koscher

Finishing Line Press
Georgetown, Kentucky

Liquid Song:
a little book of longing

Copyright © 2020 by Adeline Carrie Koscher
ISBN 978-1-64662-165-1 First Edition
All rights reserved under International and Pan-American Copyright Conventions. No part of this book may be reproduced in any manner whatsoever without written permission from the publisher, except in the case of brief quotations embodied in critical articles and reviews.

ACKNOWLEDGMENTS

I am grateful to *Novelty Magazine* for previously publishing "Swimming in Moonlight" from this chapbook.
Finishing Line Press for investing in my poetry.
My mom for encouraging me to have faith that my writing could reach an audience.
My dad for not panicking too much about my publicly airing intimate thoughts.
Scottie for reading my poems and encouraging me in the process.
Betty Ann and Carol for their wisdom and enduring encouragement of my writing pursuits.
Reade for reading my poems over the years and for quelling my anxiety over sharing my poems with the bartender.
Margaret for telling me that any man would be flattered to have these poems written about him.
Siân for reveling in the poetry of the world with me.
My sweet, sweet friends, Beth, Nico, and Nayanika, for their ebullient and sincere joy at my success in this endeavor.
The Fine Arts Work Center for providing a supportive, challenging space for writers to grow.
Paul for the inspiration, the company, and the dreams. And for being.
The Squealing Pig.
Provincetown.

Publisher: Leah Maines
Editor: Christen Kincaid
Cover Art: Betsy Koscher
Author Photo: Mariia Watts
Cover Design: Elizabeth Maines McCleavy

Printed in the USA on acid-free paper.
Order online: www.finishinglinepress.com
   also available on amazon.com

Author inquiries and mail orders:
Finishing Line Press
P. O. Box 1626
Georgetown, Kentucky 40324
U. S. A.

Table of Contents

Wingspan 1

Flying at night, ... 2

Liquid Song: both more and less than Whitman and Kunitz 4

Wanderlust 5

Celestial Mechanics 7

Everywhere Bar 9

Aphrodisiac 10

Fire in the Palm of Your Hand 11

Swimming in Moonlight 12

Just Thought I'd Let You Know (not after Bukowski) 14

Enough 16

Waking 18

This: 19

deadly serious: Robbins in Winterson 20

Nights, ... 22

Morning: 23

for Paul

"It's all I have to bring today—
This, and my heart beside—"
~Emily Dickinson

Wingspan

Perched behind the bar,
you reach from one end
to the other: your wingspan
stretches from Mountain Sun
to Glenfiddich, your center eclipses
the Blue Moon, your arms open
you to my fancy.

My hand vanishes inside yours,
expands and contracts at once—
a chestnut burr, cracked open,
fleshy center exposed. I am small, and
I am not small—I contain multitudes.

You are not a bird of prey, and I am not
a scuttlefish, field mouse, cricket. I am not
prey. I repeat all the way here:
I am predator, not prey.
Past moons I have been, but
no longer sought after,
swooped upon, snatched up. I am

predator, not prey;
predator, not prey, I am
well within your reach
on this sandbar, and consumed
with the thought of coupling—
lacing fingers and legs,
folding bodies and breath.

One fluid gesture draws your wings
to your long body—grace and ease,
breath and longing. I am stung
with my own venom—
predator and prey.

Flying at night,

rising, weightless, above
the queens of Commercial Street,
above The Pig, above the ships
in Provincetown Harbor,
above Cape Cod Bay.
Rising on breeze, sea mist
kissed; swelling in the chest,
warming in the center.
Fingers and toes tingling,
disappear—no body remains—
just breath and warmth
and a surge of sea air
through what used to be me.

The Jungians claim this flight
is arousal. Flying, they say,
suggests spiritual elation—
the dreamer touching
her own immortality. I've flown
many nights—unfettered—
one with the fog
and the lighthouse beacon.

But tonight, I watch your hands
hold my glass, wipe the bar,
rub your neck, pour scotch,
make change. When I finally land,
heavy, under a low blanket of clouds,
I dream of your hands wrapped around
my hips, around my waist—not a tether,
but a launch. Your hands, twice mine, lift me
like a ballerina, lift me like a lover, and I hover
over Commercial Street, The Pig,
Provincetown Harbor—your hands:
a pair of wings on my back.

Above Cape Cod Bay I rise on your breath—
sour with cigarettes, sweet with whiskey.
Full of breath and breathless, I rise,
swelling in the chest, warming
in the center. Fingers and toes
disappear—no body,
just breath and warmth
and a surge of sea air
through what used to be me.

Liquid Song:
> *both more and less than Whitman and Kunitz*
> *(found poem)*

The expression of a well-made man,
disgraced and mortal,
appears not only in his face.
The mercy of time
is in the limbs and joints also.
Belly to belly, it is curiously
the tropic of desire, and you
are stranded on the rocks.
In the joints of his hips and wrists:
the phosphorescence in your wake.
His walk, the carriage of his neck:
swimming in the moon.
In the flex of his waist and knees:
nobility of form.
Dress does not hide him,
pure energy incarnate.
The strong sweet quality he has—
almost imperceptible undulation—
strikes through cotton and broadcloth,
both more and less than human.
To see him pass conveys as much
sorrow without name
as the best poem, perhaps more.
In the vast loveliness of the sea,
you linger to see his back—liquid song—
and the back of his neck, crackling with life.

Wanderlust

1.   Mapping

From here, I survey the terrain, measure the topography of your contours, estimate the width of the gorge in your breast. I judge the altitude of the tallest fear, monitor storm and calm on your face, study the tides, note the effect of moon. I learn the history of this land through words and silences, pinpoint the location of the wellspring of joy, and mark the latitude of pine grove where the pale-eyed blackbird dwells. From this distance, I try echo-sounding your depths, but all, all is speculation; mapmakers are given to conjecture. Travelers become restless to crest the mountain, to swim the ocean—while dreaming of the faraway land, as I do.

2.   Traveling

Dreaming of this land, as I do, I measure the short distance from here to you—a narrow strait to ford. I could swim, paddle, leap from stone to stone, this river, this creek, this trickle, this squiggle on a map. If the wind were right, I am sure I could fly across the space between my shifting sands and the sheer cliffs of you. I will forget lives I have lost crossing these waters. I will abandon map and manual, discard compass and sextant. I will lose my way.

3.   Wandering

I lose my way, sink into the valley behind your ear, walk the ridge of your jawbone, collarbone, hipbone, linger in the hollow of your knees. I taste the briny oyster of your mouth, savor each finger, wrist, elbow hinge, get drunk on the forest musk of your skin. I dance to the ancient drumming of your pulse, then, sweaty and exhausted, as the fire dwindles, rest, until morning, at the base of your spine. I learn the language of your breath, the dialect of your laugh, the idiom of gesture. I hear every sorrow song of the dead, hidden in the ferny shadow of lashes. I sink beneath the surface of your eyes, dive into the lightless cavern of your thorax, pause at the apex of your heart—the whole world of you swirling round.

4.   Adapting

Here, with the world of you swirling round—in this foreign land, where the known no longer makes sense—leagues from my familiar, where I cannot see my own hand—amid the flora and fauna of your mind, where I have forgotten my tongue—in a moment of brilliant blindness, I learn to breathe underwater.

5.   Departing

I breathe underwater. I stand at the edge of myself, waiting. A promise presses inside my chest: I will savor, not steal; I will touch, not take. Still, my scent will linger in your caves; my impression will remain in the field, long after I have risen; and a thread of my song, transparent as spider's silk, will weave itself among every branch of every tree, forever changing the landscape of you. I will depart with only your seeds on my skirts, your breath in my lungs, my lips and cheeks dusted red with your earth, and my neck and shoulders kissed copper with your sun.

Celestial Mechanics

Across the room, I watch
you trace a small circle with your thumb,
round and around and around—

drawing my consciousness.
Your shoulders curve, neck curls
over fluid, concentric, pulses.

This revolution moves through
your arm, through muscle and sinew,
through shoulder, neck, chin, jaw.

My vision clouds: the gravitational force
of one celestial body on another—
ample resistance, ample pressure—

a balance of weight and weightlessness.
Paralyzed by the possibility of your hand
cupping, your thumb circling—

dissipation of kinetic energy rippling
concentric through my watery center
through my shoulders, neck, tongue, lips—

my fingertips trace the pulse along
your wrist, forearm, bicep, shoulder, along
your collarbone, neck, chin, jaw into your hair.

My hungry-bird mouth demands yours: I draw
you in and in and in, until we begin to balance
between weight and weightlessness.

This small gesture circumscribes a space
between reality and possibility. My mouth—
a small circle—opens and closes

at the thought of your thumb gilding
a ring around the blood moon.
Across the surface tension of this room,

a shrinking circle hovers, draws us closer
and closer, opening and closing, contracting
the space between us, radiating a tidal force.

Across the room, I watch
you trace a silvery ring
around the blood moon.

Everywhere Bar

I go to the bar, that's a bar in St. Andrews, but it's also The Pig and every other bar I've ever worked at or been to. And you are behind the bar, and you are you but also all the bartenders I've ever fallen for—Dougie and Jaimie and John. We're close. We're at this everywhere bar where I used to work but I don't anymore, and we're close—physically close to each other—and we're close—inwardly close to each other. You're cleaning the bar, and I say something you don't quite hear so you lean over a little—even though you don't have to, because you don't have to hear me to know me—but you lean over; your tall body that hinges high brings you closer. And I just stand up on the rung of my barstool and lay one on you. I just put a big ol' smacker right on your kisser, and you let me, you let me kiss you, you let me kiss you sweet and long. And then I'm walking down Bridge Street, all of a sudden just walking down Bridge Street, and I'm barely touching the ground, and I think to myself, why am I not flying? And so, I just fly. I just rise up off the ground, and I fly down Bridge Street, fly all around old St. Andrews.

Aphrodisiac

In the center, cocoa swirls: dizzying
infusions of passion fruit and honey,
buttery air, thick with cream and oil,
golden sheen on molded confections,
hovering sweetness, light on my tongue.

I'm allergic to chocolate;
indulgence gives me hives.

This liqueur—
           too strong to resist,
           too divine to contain—

I binge,
      besotted,
                in spite of myself.

Fire in the Palm of Your Hand

Enough light? you ask,
drawing up a little red lantern.
You ignite my page.

Your broad hand
cups the flame.
You rest another
before me.

If I stayed all night,
would you surround me
with glowing jars,
bottled heat? I redden.

You place one by my pen:
deliver flickers,
illuminate my line.

You surround me in tiny fires
so numerous that
this room vanishes.

Only your hands
and my face remain,
licked into light.

I burn: a little red lantern,
devouring your breath.
You bring me fire
in the palm of your hand.

Swimming in Moonlight

You call my bluff,
No one's afraid of swimming.
Drowning, maybe. Not swimming.
You are right. I am released
by water—I become water,
freed from my solid self,
from this vessel for the soul.
It's something else I'm afraid of.

At seven, I swam until bedtime.
At seventeen, I dove from the tip of summer,
as far into the center as my lungs would allow—
At twenty-seven, I began a slow crawl
from shore to shore—a steady, rhythmic,
watery meditation: stroke, stroke, breathe,
stroke, stroke, breathe. I have been
swimming across ever since.

There's something else I'm afraid of.
Somewhere, between strokes and breaths,
snappers surfaced; fear dressed itself
in their ancient bodies. You say,
they don't bother you in the water;
they hide. They snap on shore,
when vulnerable. Your eyes dilate
with the night, hold me.

I am drawn to the water at midnight,
I take off the skin of the world,
walk into the pond, lighter than ever,
I see myself shimmering in blue—
moon and water and woman are one.
I slip under the surface, reemerge—
I never feel more beautiful
than when I'm swimming naked
in the moonlight.

You strip away my fear. It falls,
a silky puddle at my feet. I step
out, as if it never hung
on my shoulders. In this world,
some fear is good. It keeps us
from exposing our fleshy center,
our soft belly. It protects us
from what would pierce us,
tear us open, leave us drowning.
I am drawn back to the water, night
after night, aching to swim longer,
stay later—less guarded every time,
diving blind into the mystery, surfacing
in watery radiance. Safe, free:
sometimes we sacrifice one
for the other. You bring me
into moonlight,
into the water.

Just Thought I'd Let You Know
(not after Bukowski)

This is not a love poem
because I am not Bukowski, and
I am not a racehorse bet with good odds.
I do not drink or smoke,
and I have never taken a trip
that did not require luggage.

This is not a love poem
because I am a teacher, and
I do not have the body
of a twentyearold stripper
or a twentydollar whore.
I drive a Prius. I have a cat. I drink tea.

This is not a love poem
because I have never watched
The Big Lebowski, I know nothing
about beer, I can spend a whole day
in the garden without realizing,
I *like* glitter, I listen to folk music.

This is not a love poem
because I have not read Tom Robbins
or Hunter S. Thompson; I hate Kerouac—
and *all* the Beats, for that matter.
Because I am sorry for your wife.
I am sorry for everybody's wife.

This is not a love poem
because you are not my type.
I like small men, my size,
with dark hair and light eyes,
men who do not flirt
when they are engaged.

This is not a love poem
because I am content with
conversation, with cranberry and soda,
content to ring the devil's doorbell
and imagine my hands
are yours. I tell myself:

This is not a love poem
because I am trying to hold on,
but my heart is a slippery bugger—
squirming, gills flaring.
Gasping, it will not be held.
Just thought I'd let you know, fucker.

Enough

I think, *it'll be enough*. I tell myself, *it is enough, just this*. I tell myself, *this grain of pleasure is all I need*. And it is—for the time being. I can lessen the longing if I feed it a little. A little nourishment takes the edge off.

But the hunger grows. Proximity no longer satisfies. Being in the same room whets my appetite. I long for more. I take a little more, just a little: an ear, a finger. I take it home with me. I roll it in the palm of my memory. I linger sensate on that morsel of flesh. And it satisfies, for a time. It fills me, buoys me from depths to surface and into the air. I float on the trickle of a laugh, the flex of a thumb.

In time, my gossamer-self becomes solid again. Flesh-and-bone feet settle on the earth. And my heart sinks heavy into my gut, into my hips, until I'm dragging it along behind me attached to a leg iron I cannot file. It carves a path in the earth, marking each step I labor to take. I weary from walking. I sit. I fear I might not get up. I might sink into the earth, weighted by my cumbersome heart.

But I don't sink into the earth; I don't fold into myself like a moonflower at dawn. A brisk morning breeze catches one of my corners: a square still untattered. The day whisks me back to the source of joy. And I feed again, grow strong, mend, heal. Your philosophies fix my frayed edges. Your confessions flood my flesh. My cheeks redden; my pulse quickens. You smile, you scowl, you smirk: and it is enough.

I tell myself, *it is enough*. It will last me. I can savor these. I capture them in my net, pin them to my specimen board, still squirming with life, ebullient. I keep them as my own—though, they never were. I possess them, study them, visit them daily—these fluttering parts of you.

It is enough, for a time. Then, they fade, they droop, they become hardened carcasses—empty shells. Lifeless, chalky—if I breathe too close to them, they become dust, become air, disappear altogether.

I am careful. I visit them less; treat them as precious antiquities. They keep me alive in spite of their fading. One day I return to the little pinboard to find only shadows of what was once tacked there—the cork around their lithe souls faded in daylight; the cork beneath them darker, richer for their having rested upon it.

I begin to forget their fleecy texture; the tiny, percussive rhythm of their wings. I long for the clarity of that memory, the renewal it offered. And I return to you, wasted, wan. I sit on your doorstep in the rain, waiting, because I cannot feel the rain or the sun. I feel only longing, only the deepest need for one more word, one more conversation, maybe the slightest touch.

If not a touch, maybe a look—one look, held just a moment longer than is discrete. If not that, just stand near enough so I may feel the warmth of your pulsing being. Just near enough for me to siphon a bit of your liquid light to burn in my lantern through the darkest winter nights. This will be enough. This, this will be enough.

Waking

Last night, I dreamt
of an abundance of peppers,
of swimming whole days with Carissa,
of a hurricane coming, of rooms made of glass.
I dreamt my mother moved all the furniture and
hung her nightgowns outside the closet: shapeless,
oversized, terrycloth tents. I dreamt of growing seedlings
in egg cartons, of traveling with my grandma, staying
at the wrong hotel, a hotel without a name. No one
knew it: not the concierge, the bellhop, none
of the guests, no locals. I dreamt of packing,
clearing belongings from under the bed—
so many forgotten: some mine,
some not mine—left by
another traveler.

I am wakened by neighbors'
rumble-rattle of coming and going,
clunk-clack of opening and closing—
each sound of arrival brings you here: into
my home, into my consciousness, into my bed.
Waking, I dream of your hands: one presses the small
of my back, one cups my shoulder, one cradles my breast,
one lifts my face, one on my soft belly, one under my thigh,
one in my hair, one behind my neck. Only one, only one
hand fits on my body at once, so large are your hands:
your hands usher me from that world to this.

Your hands lift me from the weight of sleep,
from a plague of dreams; lift me from yesterday,
lift me from fear, from guilt, from worry,
from him, from them, from then,
your hands carry me into today,
like something worthy of
this morning, of this
possibility.

This:

because
you cannot nap, can't sleep much at all,
because you say a boy should grow
the longest wildest hair he can,
because, exasperated, your voice
climbs an octave, because you protect
the queer souls of this queer town,
because you are shadow and light,
flickering in one tall hurricane lamp.

because
I deny myself precious sleep
to know you, because your words
nest in my hair—a whorl of thought
and sunlight, wilding against the night—
because the warm kiss of your hand
on the small of my back spins
through me, tugs loose all my anchors,
bewilders my own queer soul.

because
in slumber or not, the very thought
of you—your voice in my hair,
your tender care of the lost
the wayward, your calm and storm—
softens me, warms me, finds me
swelling, rising, under a moist
gingham cloth, by a sunny window,
waiting for your hands to return.

deadly serious:
>*Robbins in Winterson*
>*(found poem)*

i.
I had a name
but I have forgotten it.
So it is for us, the eclipse:
the presence of love
on earth in these suits of lead,
transported to another plane—
not far away, but too far to touch.

Was I searching?
Did it make your brown eyes blue—
the dancing part of myself?

ii.
The marvelous, the stream—
precisely unthinkable—
bottom-crowded with tiny pebbles
that must be thought:

A bartender's beauty—
sides sprouting watercress—
furious delicacy, like a lover.
There is a rock near to its source:

power contained like a matador's in peace,
singing songs of love and death. I hide
behind it at evening, waiting to dissolve
at any moment, in the way you move.

iii.
Light burns out into the street
reaches in our bodies,
scratches the cobblestones
for a choice made in secret:
chestnut blossoms
against the blackboard of the sky.

Feathers fly out of pillows,
after nights of longing. A shaping spirit:
rarely is the beloved more than
the teapot song of the lover's dreams.
Perhaps such a thing is enough, between
rosebushes and the pistachio tree.

Nights,

I wake, flushed,
a ripe honey apple,
in your dream hand.

Heavy in your palm,
rosy curves,
swollen with wanting.

You hold me between
what is permitted
and what is forbidden.
I glow with possibility,

draw your eye. I blush and swell,
blush and swell, fitting myself in
the well of your hand, weighing
more with each turn.

Morning:

Imagine you wake from sleeplessness
to discover you no longer need sleep;
you need conversation in a look,
laughter in a shoulder—
they are your eggs and bacon,
toast and jam.

This truth: sure
as one breath will follow
another; familiar
as the taste of water,
the sound of rain.
Knowing and glassy-eyed,
you look out, above the tall pines.

This knowing
is the color
of sunrise.

This collection of poems was born out of the madness of longing one steamy August. When Carrie delivered a tiny, hand-stitched version to the subject of the poems, he responded, "Wait, I'm your fucking muse?"

At the heart of much of Carrie's creative and scholarly work is an examination of how women become more in touch with themselves and how they engage the world. She finds writing a way to accomplish both.

Carrie's poetry often dips into prose, and her prose into poetry. Likewise, in her writing the line between reality and dreams is blurred. Her writing is influenced by the dream life we experience both awake and asleep.

Carrie earned her Ph.D. from the University of St. Andrews in Scotland. Her dissertation: *The New Woman Novelist and the Redefinition of the Female: Marriage, Sexuality, and Motherhood* examines women writers of the fin de siècle and their influence on the evolving experience of women in society. Her scholarly interests center on women, memory, and sexuality.

In 2017, Carrie's poem "Boiling Potatoes While Listening to Public Radio" was chosen by Marge Piercy as the regional winner of the Joe Gouveia Outermost Poetry Contest. Carrie's poems, essays, and stories can be found in *Review Americana, The Lyon Review, Adana, Altered States, ninepatch, Zetetic, Claudius Speaks, Canary, Novelty Magazine*, and in the upcoming anthology *From the Farther Shore*.

www.ingramcontent.com/pod-product-compliance
Lightning Source LLC
LaVergne TN
LVHW041519070426
835507LV00012B/1685